THE KINGFISHER TREASURY OF
MYTHS AND LEGENDS

For Uncle Ken and all his loved ones—A. P.

For Trevor—K. M. D.

KINGFISHER
a Houghton Mifflin Company imprint
222 Berkeley Street
Boston, Massachusetts 02116
www.houghtonmifflinbooks.com

First published in hardcover in 1993
First published in paperback in 2003
2 4 6 8 10 9 7 5 3 1

LIBRARY OF CONGRESS CATALOGING-IN-PUBLICATION DATA
has been applied for.

ISBN 0-7534-5635-4

Printed in Taiwan

1TR/0203/SHE/–/126.6MA

THE KINGFISHER TREASURY OF
MYTHS AND LEGENDS

ANN PILLING

ILLUSTRATED BY
KADY MacDONALD DENTON

KINGFISHER
BOSTON

Contents

Fools and Heroes

INTRODUCTION

The question most often asked of a writer is this: "When you begin a book, what is your most useful starting point?" My own answer never varies. It is, "A good story to tell." And these are hard to come by. If you should ever find one, guard it carefully. It is precious, like gold.

When he traveled in "the realms of gold" John Keats was looking for great poems. To make this book I have been traveling too, but on the lookout for good stories. And here they are, fourteen tales from many peoples, and from many lands.

All the stories in this book are "good," and they have proved themselves over hundreds, sometimes thousands, of years. The people that first heard them would not let them go, but carried them around like some special treasure. Very often they couldn't read, so the stories were passed on "orally," by word of mouth. Some would be told around the campfire, some to while away a long journey, others at a grandmother's knee. Because they were passed down from one generation to another, they changed. Some bits got lost and new bits were added. Names altered and so did places. That is why, in putting this collection together, I often read several versions of the same story before wrapping my own words around it.

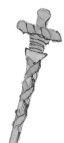

But a truly *great* story does not depend on the "wrapping." If we think of *Persephone*, one of the most haunting and beautiful stories in this collection, we realize that its power does not really depend on how I tell it. It could be told in a few simple

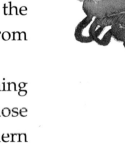

sentences, or as a long elaborate poem, or as grand opera. However such a tale is told, we will be moved by it because of what it is *in itself*.

In this book the stories are grouped around common themes. There are myths that answer questions about the natural world: Where did fire come from? Why are the moon and stars in the sky? Then come deeper legends about love and death: *Balder*, with all its beauty and heartbreak; *Bedd Gelert*, the story of a dog's sacrifice. Finally we meet both fools and heroes: *Midas* with his greed for gold, the two Irish giants who couldn't swim, *Perseus*, the supreme adventurer.

Each story has its own peculiar wisdom and poetry. How is it that these ancient tales still have such power over us, when the worlds and ways of life reflected in them are so different from our own?

I think it is because, at the heart of each, there is something that speaks to us, often with great simplicity, about those things that do not change. C. S. Lewis, himself a modern myth-maker, once said that myth was perhaps "an unfocussed gleam of human imagination falling on divine truth."

"A good poem begins in delight and ends in wisdom." This is equally true of a good story. My hope is that in this book you will find both delight and wisdom, and may you get as much pleasure from the reading as I have from the telling.

Ann Pilling

IYADOLA'S BABIES

A West African Myth

Nyame, the great sky god, was lonely up in the clouds, so one day he made a huge round basket and filled it with animals, with insects and birds. When it was ready, he cut a big hole in the sky, a curved hole like a slice of orange. Then he pushed the basket through, stretched out his hand, and hung it on a cloud. So he could see it better, he cut some little pointed holes to let the light through. These were the stars, and the big curved one was the moon.

For a while Nyame was happy, looking down at his big round basket, which he had called Earth, but then he got bored. So he made another basket, filled it with flowers and plants, then sprinkled them all over Earth through the orange-shaped hole.

He was pleased with it now, and he spent long happy days watching the animals coming and going on Earth, watching the blossoms come out, the grass grow long and lush. But others were watching too, for inside Nyame lived two little spirit people, a man and a woman, and they sometimes crept right to the edge of the sky god's mouth and peeped out.

One day Nyame caught a bad cold and gave a terrific sneeze. Out fell the spirit people, through the big curved hole in the clouds, and down, down, down until they landed on Earth with a bump.

What a funny place it was, after the comfortable warm

darkness inside Nyame! They wandered all over it, looking at the trees and the flowers. They watched the animals playing and the insects scurrying busily about; they marveled at the rain, at the wind and the sun. Soon the man spirit found that he could catch the animals with sharp sticks, and he became a hunter.

Iyadola, the woman spirit, grew lonely then. Her man didn't want her to come hunting with him; he left her all alone, in the cave where they had made their home. So one day she worked out a plan, and when he came back that night she was eager to tell him all about it.

He didn't want to listen though. "I don't like your plans," he said grumpily. "It was your plan to creep into Nyame's mouth, to see what he was doing. If it hadn't been for you we'd still be safe and warm, not stranded on Earth getting hungry, with me having to hunt for our food."

But Iyadola was determined to explain. "We could get some clay," she said, "and we could make some little creatures that looked just like us. We could bake them in the fire and breathe life into them, so that they could walk and talk, like we do. They could be our children. If they were with me I wouldn't be so lonely when you went off hunting all day."

The man spirit had to agree that this was a fine idea, so the very next day they got busy. They heaped up the fire till it glowed red hot and made a whole batch of little clay children, putting them carefully into the bright embers so they would cook properly. Then they sat back and waited excitedly to see what would happen next.

What happened was that Nyame came thundering through the trees, shouting out their names in his enormous, deep voice. They were frightened of the great sky god and they snatched their little clay children out of the fire, wrapping them in cool leaves in case he saw what they'd been up to. He was a moody kind of god, and they thought he might punish them.

But he only wanted to see how they liked Earth, with all its plants and animals, its creeping things, its rivers, and its rainbows. He was a god who liked praise. "We love it, Nyame," they said in chorus, bowing low before him; and he went away content.

The minute he was out of sight they made some more children and put them in the fire, but they'd scarcely wiped the clay off their hands before Nyame came crashing back. "I hope you're behaving yourselves, here on Earth," he said self-importantly. "I made it, you know. I expect you to look after it. By the way, what's this great fire for?" And he poked at it suspiciously.

"We were cold, Nyame," they said, feeling rather foolish, for the sun was shining.

"Humph!" snorted the sky god, and away he went again. He had stayed so long that the second batch of clay children were all but ruined.

All day the two little spirits baked busily, but Nyame, who clearly thought he was missing something, kept coming back to check up on them. Sometimes, when they heard his footsteps, they had to whip the clay babies out before they were ready. Sometimes, he just wouldn't go away, with the result that the batch was overcooked.

In the end, though, the sky god got hungry and went back home for good. As soon as they felt it was safe, the spirit people unwrapped all the green leaves, set out their handiwork on the forest floor and looked at it.

Some of the children hadn't been in the fire nearly long enough and they were almost white. Others had been in far too long, while Nyame was busy talking, and these had been burned black. There were lots of other colors too, yellow and red-brown, and pink.

Iyadola was delighted, and she swept them all up in her arms. With the help of the spirit man she breathed warm life into them and soon they stretched, wiggled their new little legs, and ran around the forest. After that, she no longer complained when the man sharpened his sticks and went hunting. She would never be lonely again; she had her children. And that is why she is called "Iyadola" because it means "Earth Mother."

NAMING THE WINDS

An Iroquois Myth
from North America

Ga-oh the giant lives far away, up in the sky. From Earth he looks quite small, but in fact he is the biggest of all the giants, and the most powerful. For at the beginning of time Ga-oh named the Four Winds, and he rules them still.

First he called Bear to him, Bear whose huge shaggy paws scooped out valleys as he lumbered along, heaping up the earth into towering mountain ranges. "Bear," said the god, "you are surely the strongest of all. You have only to blow a little and the rivers turn to ice. Wherever you go men shiver and shake, making big fires to keep you away. It is always winter with you. Be my great North Wind, and command my herd of winter gales, when I set them free."

So Bear bowed his head before Ga-oh, and the god slipped a strong leash around his neck. Then he bounded off to take his place in the far north of the sky where he sat growling and making thunder, waiting for Ga-oh's next command.

The god called again, to Fawn. His voice was very different this time, low and soft, the voice of water rippling over little stones. Nervously, the creature came to him, and with her came birdsong, and the sweet smell of blossom.

"Fawn," said Ga-oh, stroking her neck as she bowed before him, "you are gentle and lovely. Be my South Wind, and watch over my flock of summer breezes." Over her head he slipped silken reins, then he sent her away to the

15

south of the sky where she browsed peacefully among the clouds, waiting until he should summon her back to him.

West Wind was next, and he was a great black panther. As he came leaping through the sky to answer the giant's call, he split the clouds apart with a great snarling, and his bare claws rent them into shreds. "What is your command, great Ga-oh?" he said, and his sleek, dark coat threw black shadows on the sun, as he bowed before the giant.

"Panther," said Ga-oh, "you are fierce and very strong. You shall be my maker of storms. Nothing can heap up the waves or blow hurricanes like you; all men will tremble when you howl your warning over the sky. Be gone. You are my wild West Wind." And Panther crept away, pulling impatiently at the strong black leash with which the giant had tied him, and snarling angrily. He could hardly wait to wreak havoc on the earth with one of his storms.

The fourth corner of the sky was still empty, so Ga-oh lifted up his voice and called for the very last time. Moose came crashing through the forest with a pounding of hoofs and a battering of great antlers. "Moose," said the giant, slipping a rope around his neck, "wherever you are there is rain and fog. Be my damp East Wind, the wind that brings drizzle and wet," and he sent Moose off to the chilly reaches of the eastern sky.

Then Ga-oh, tired with his summoning of winds, went back to the highest part of the heavens and sat there resting, with the four leashes in his hand.

And he sits there still. But he is a moody god. Only when he is happy will he release Fawn, letting her waft warm breezes over the earth. More often he frees Bear, who makes terrible storms, or Panther, who snarls and bites. Sometimes Moose is given his freedom too. Then it rains and blows, sending men scurrying for shelter, barring their doors against the blast.

Sometimes, when he is feeling more peaceful, he keeps tight hold of all four winds, of Panther and Moose, of Bear and of Fawn. Then the sun comes out, the birds start singing, and here on Earth we know that Ga-oh the giant is having a happy day.

HOW MAUI STOLE FIRE FROM THE GODS

A Myth from the Pacific Islands

There was a time when people had no fire on earth, no fire to warm themselves or to give them light when the darkness came, and no fire to cook with. Maui became famous as the boy who got fire from the gods. He was only young, but he was clever and brave, and this is his story.

It came about because his mother, Harva, who sometimes visited the gods, came back one day with some delicious food. When Maui tasted it his mouth watered, and he begged for more. "Why is it different?" he said. "Why does it taste so much better than any other food?"

"It has been cooked," explained Harva, "in a pot, over a slow fire."

"Why didn't you bring fire back with you?" said Maui.

"Because fire is guarded by the giant Mahuika, and he will never part with it. Nothing, not so much as a single coal, will he give to the people on earth."

"Then I will steal it," Maui announced boldly.

His mother laughed. "He will crush you to pieces," she said. "If I were you I'd stay here, and eat cold food."

But the next time Harva went visiting, Maui followed her in secret. It was a long, hard journey, but at last she stopped in front of a great wall of rock where she uttered some magic

words, making a gateway appear. She passed through, and the gates clanged shut again, and vanished.

When all was quiet Maui whispered the magic words too. At once the gates appeared in the rock, and he too went through. His mother was nowhere to be seen, but a long yellow road stretched out before him. He followed it and came at last to the house of an old man called Tane.

"I know you," said Tane. "You're Harva's son. What are you doing here?"

"I have come to steal fire from the gods," answered Maui.

The old man pulled thoughtfully at his beard. "That's dangerous," he said. "Mahuika guards it well. He will crush you into little pieces."

"I must have it," said Maui.

"Can nothing I say make you change your mind, and go home again?"

"Nothing. I must have fire," repeated Maui.

So, to help him, Tane gave him a red dove called Fearless, and told him a magic spell. "Say it when you reach the Gorge of Demons," he said. "You will be in great danger when you enter that terrible valley. The spell will turn you into a dragonfly. Follow Fearless and she will lead you to the house of banyan logs where Mahuika sits, guarding his fire. Go, my son, and may the blessings of the gods go with you." And he turned back sadly into his house.

So Maui set off, with the red dove flying before him, and came at last to the Gorge of Demons. There he uttered Tane's magic words and was at once changed into a dragonfly, which rose shimmering into the air. As they flew through the valley, demon hands reached out to clutch at

them, trying to grasp them and squeeze them to death with fiery fingers. But they zig-zagged from left to right, while the demons hissed at them in anger, and at last reached the end of the valley in safety, where Maui instantly became a boy again.

There before him was the house of banyan logs, with Fearless fluttering bravely over the roof. In front of it sat the giant Mahuika, guarding his fire.

"Who are you?" he roared.

"I am Maui, from Earth," the boy said boldly.

"And how did you get through the valley of demons?" The giant was astonished. Nothing had ever survived the terrible journey before.

"That's my secret," said Maui. "But if you show me the secret of fire I shall tell you."

So Mahuika, thinking the boy was foolish, gave him a bit of burning wood out of the flames. "There," he said slyly, knowing that the wood would burn away to nothing long before Maui reached home. "You have fire. Now tell me your secret."

But Maui knew that the giant was trying to trick him, so he waited until the piece of wood had burned away. Then Mahuika gave him a dish of glowing embers, but Maui threw them into some water, where they too went out, with a hiss.

At this the giant got angry, gave Maui a pot of ashes and shouted, "Be gone, or I'll tear you to pieces!" But Maui simply threw the ashes into Mahuika's eyes, so that he couldn't see.

In vain the giant blundered around, trying to grab at the

boy, but Maui danced out of reach, taunting him. "I could kill you now," he said. "I could throw burning sticks all over you and send you up in smoke. But if you give me the secret of fire I will spare your life."

"I will fight you for it," moaned Mahuika, washing the ash from his eyes, and with one quick dart he swept Maui from the ground and tucked him into his belt.

But the boy merely puffed out his chest, snapped the belt in two and said boastfully, "I won that round. Now then, let's try throwing. I can throw higher than you."

"Never," said the giant and tossed him into the air, but Maui came down again, almost at once. The second throw was better, but after a while, Maui came bouncing back.

With a roar Mahuika flung him up yet again, and this time he stayed in the air so long that the giant had time to sing a whole song :

> "Up you go to the first level!
> Up you go to the second level!
> Up you go to the third level!
> Up you go to the fourth level!
> Up you go to the fifth level!
> Up you go to the sixth level!
> Up you go to the seventh level!
> Up you go to the eighth level!
> Up you go to the ninth level!
> Up you go to the tenth level!"

Then the giant stared up at the sky in amazement. For he had finished his song, but Maui was still paddling about over his head. He was enjoying himself.

"Drop, can't you, *drop*!" Mahuika bellowed, and at last Maui came floating back to earth, roaring with laughter.

"That's that, then," said the giant. "I'm an elephant compared to you, you won't move me an inch. Fire is safe with me." But hardly had he finished speaking when he found himself hurtling through the air. Maui's first throw got him as far as the coconut tree, his second as far as the date palm. The third sent him so high that the boy had time to sing the Song of the Levels all through, twice, and still Mahuika didn't return to earth.

"Let me come down, I beg of you!" wailed the giant. He was frightened now. This was no ordinary boy, but a demon. "What will you give me, if I bring you back to earth?" shouted Maui.

"Anything," Mahuika shouted back, "just let me come down, and catch me, or I'll be squashed to a pulp."

"Promise you'll show me the secret of fire," said the wily Maui.

"I promise." The giant's voice was now faint and far away, he had gone up so high.

So the boy caught him, just as if he were a feather, and Mahuika stormed into his house of banyan logs and came out with two fire-sticks. One was round and the other was flat, with a little hollow in the middle.

Maui watched carefully as the giant put the round stick into the hollow, twirling it round and round till a spark leaped out, then a tongue of flame. Blowing it out, he put the fire-sticks in the boy's hands. "You have fire," he said. "Mahuika has kept his promise. Go in safety through the Gorge of Demons. They have no power to hurt you now."

So, with Fearless flying ahead of him, Maui returned with his fire-sticks to the world of men. And fire became a servant to the people on earth, and a friend. They could cook food with it and warm themselves with it too; they could soften metals with it, and bake bricks in it. At night they could use it to frighten away the wild animals, and when they sat by their fires they sometimes sang the Song of the Levels, in memory of the marvelous boy who had thrown the giant into the air.

The gods were angry with Mahuika for giving a human child the secret of fire, and they punished him. But Maui always praised him, because he had fought a good fight.

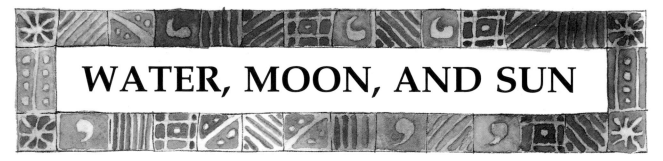

WATER, MOON, AND SUN

A Nigerian Myth

Long, long ago Sun married Moon, and for a while they were very happy together, and very busy setting up house. But the time came when they wanted to see their friends again, and their very best friend was Water.

"Hey!" Sun called to him, across the earth. "What about paying us a visit? It's a long time since we saw you."

"I'd love to come," Water called back, in his deep gurgling voice, "but can I bring my friends? There are a lot of them, I'm afraid. I think your new house will be too small for us."

"Not at all," said Sun. "We'll build a whole new village, with dozens of huts and a big fence all around, to keep out the wild animals. That's it, we'll build a special kraal, just for you. Do say you'll come. We miss you."

So Water agreed, and set off to visit Sun and Moon. With him went all the creatures in the sea, the tiny sardines and the massive whales, the razor-toothed sharks and the glowing rainbow fish, the crabs and the lobsters.

Sun and Moon were excited. They could hear Water's great

roaring miles away, long before they could see him. Then they spotted him, flowing like a broad blue ribbon around the hills and through the forests, then charging, broader and mightier still, across the thirsty plains. At last he swirled in, covering their feet.

"It's wonderful to see you again, dear friends," he boomed, "and what a marvelous new village you've built."

"Er, yes," Moon said rather nervously, as Water and his friends swished about, exploring every corner of the kraal, and a crab took a sly nip at her toes.

"Is everybody here?" called Sun, above the roaring of Water. "I'm afraid we're getting rather short of space." He and Moon had already retreated outside their hut, to one corner of the kraal. The inside was useless, for all the furniture was floating around.

"Not quite," shouted Water, above the din, and in swept two whales blowing their water spouts madly, and a great big hippopotamus, which immediately squashed poor Moon against the fence. "Help!" she shouted. "You've

filled up the kraal. There's no room for anything else. Stop, Water, stop!'' But Water didn't hear her. He was much too busy welcoming all his friends. Sun and Moon looked down at the scene in alarm, at the bobbing jellyfish and the wriggling eels, at the proud sea-horses as they went riding by. Then a couple of flying fish came zipping along, and they ducked their heads.

"It's no good," wept Moon, "the kraal's full to overflowing. I'd simply no idea that Water had so many friends. We can't stay here. I'm leaving." And she took a great leap into the sky. Sun, who loved her, followed, landing even higher, and Water was left down on Earth, filling the great kraal with all his fishy friends.

And that is why there are lakes and rivers and seas all over the world, and why Sun and Moon shine down on them from up above, Sun fierce and hot by day, Moon, more gently, by night.

THE DEATH OF BALDER

A Norse Legend

Odin was the king of the gods, and Balder was his beloved son. Hoder, Balder's twin brother, was blind, the child of darkness; but Balder, most beautiful with his pale gold hair and the sun in his face, was the Shining One, the child of light. So lovely was Balder that all the white blossoms on earth were called by his name. Where he walked the birds sang "Balder! Balder!" for sheer joy at his coming. Nothing evil had ever come near the palace where he lived with his young wife, Nanna. Therefore it was called "The Place of Peace."

But a time came when Balder grew sick at heart. "Father," he confessed to the great lord Odin, "I have had dreams of death. I have seen the dark halls of the dead and Hel, their terrible queen. I have seen myself sitting among her gray and sorrowing people, with Nanna by my side."

When he heard this Odin was troubled. It meant that Balder was going to die, and he knew that this would be the beginning of Ragnarok, the Twilight of the Gods, when all things would cease. So he saddled Sleipnir, his huge eight-legged horse, and set off across Bifrost, the rainbow bridge that joins Asgard, where the gods live, to the land of men. For three days and nights he journeyed until he came to Helheim, the kingdom of the dead, where the great dog Garm barked at him savagely, barring his way.

He rode all around the towering walls of the kingdom until

he reached a field where the dead lay sleeping. There he searched among the graves until he found the name of Volva the witch. Drawing his sword, he wrote magic letters on the ground and chanted a spell. Slowly the earth broke open and Volva stood before him.

"Who wakes me?" she cried. "I who was buried in the snow and frozen in the ice for hundreds of years? Who comes to trouble my long sleep with the quiet dead?"

"It is I," said Odin, sheathing his sword. "In Asgard it is said that Balder must die. Is it true that even now they are brewing the mead for him, here in Helheim? That an empty seat stands waiting for my beloved son?"

"It is true," croaked the witch. "These things are done for Balder. Now leave me to my rest." And she sank back into the earth.

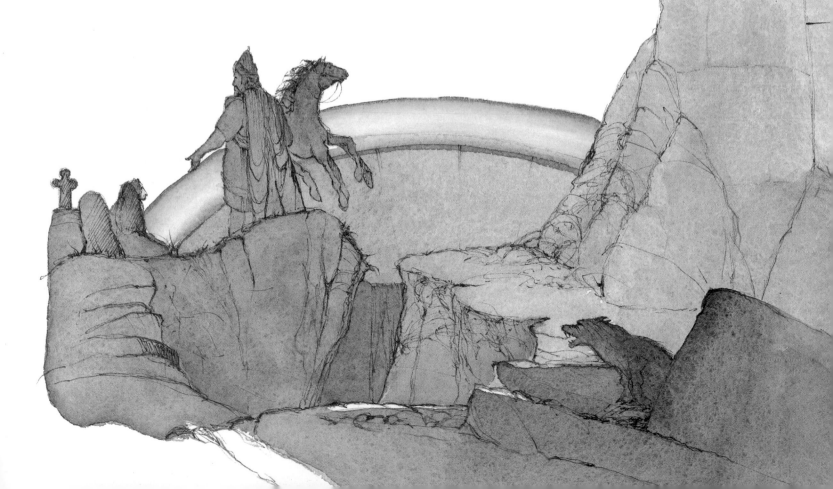

Spurring on Sleipnir, Odin rode back to Asgard with the terrible news. But Frigga, Balder's mother, did not despair. Instead, she set off on a great journey. All over the world she went, and from everything that could harm her son she took a promise, that it would never injure him. So fire promised, and water. Earth promised, and wood, and metal. The beasts promised and so did the birds. Tiny creeping things promised and great monsters of the deep promised. Disease and sickness promised, and poisons too. Nothing at all was left out. At last, weary from her wanderings, she returned to Asgard, and her face was bright. "Nothing on earth will hurt Balder now," she said.

When the young gods heard this, they made up a new game. They took Balder into Idavollr, the great meadow where they held their sports, and there they threw all manner of things at him, to see if what Frigga had told them could really be true. It was. They marveled as their darts and javelins glanced aside, leaving him untouched. Nothing they could throw could hurt him, and he laughed as the rocks and stones they hurled at him fell meekly to the earth, and rolled away.

Everybody rejoiced except Loki the Jealous. It was not right, he thought, that anyone should be so happy, so

beautiful, so well beloved. He determined then and there to end Balder's life, and to bring grief upon Odin and the other gods, whom he had always hated.

So, taking the shape of an old woman, he went to see Frigga. "Is it really true," he croaked, "that nothing on earth can hurt Balder?"

"Indeed it is," smiled the goddess. "I have taken an oath from every thing on earth. All have promised that they will never harm him."

"Every *single* thing?" said Loki. "Are you quite sure?"

"All except one," she said. "I did not trouble to speak to the mistletoe. It grows on an oak tree, to the east of Valhalla. It is such a poor creature it doesn't even have its own root, but has to draw its strength from other trees. It couldn't possibly harm him."

"No, of course not," soothed the old woman, and she hobbled away.

As soon as he was out of sight Loki resumed his own shape and hurried to the woods east of Valhalla, Odin's great gold hall where he feasted the souls of the brave. There he found the mistletoe bough. Cutting off a strong piece, he took his knife and made it into a dart. Then he sped back to Idavollr, where the gods were still playing with Balder.

Everybody was laughing and joking, except blind Hoder; the sport was no fun at all for him, because he could not see to make a throw.

"Here," said the cunning Loki, putting the sharp little dart between his empty fingers. "Why should you not join in the sport too? Let me guide your hand."

So Hoder took aim, and guided by Loki, the dart reached its goal. It struck Balder on the breast, piercing his tunic, and he sank to the ground. As the life drained away from his face it was as if a cloud had covered the sun.

Poor blind Hoder stood bewildered and alone as the gods gathered around in horror, trying to revive Balder. Nobody saw Loki slip away. The awful darkness in him had put out the light of the Shining One for ever and ever.

Frigga stepped forward and stood by the body of her son. Through her tears she begged that someone might go to the kingdom of the dead and plead with the goddess Hel to be merciful and to release Balder. "Whoever does this will have my love and my good will for ever," she said, weeping.

At this, Hermod the Swift stepped forward. "I will go," he cried, and leaping onto Sleipnir, Odin's great charger, he set off for Helheim, across the rainbow bridge.

Meanwhile the gods took up Balder and carried him to the edge of the sea where Hringhorn, his own ship, stood waiting for its beloved master. On it they built a great funeral pyre, and then they lifted up the body of the Shining One and set it in the midst. The ship was so heavy that not even Thor, the thunder god, could move it. So they summoned

Nyrrokin the giantess, who came riding to the sea on a huge wolf with snakes for its bridle. She it was who sent Hringhorn on its last journey, after each of the gods had bent over Balder, to say goodbye. When Nanna's turn came her heart burst with grief, and they laid her beside her lord as the flames of the funeral ship curled upward, blackening the sun. Then a great cry went up from all who saw it: "Balder the Beautiful is dead, is dead."

Meanwhile, brave Hermod was riding long and hard, stopping neither for food nor drink till he came to Gioll, the river of fire which flows around Helheim, the kingdom of the dead. There, on a golden bridge, Modgudur the death maiden stood on guard.

"Who rides this way?" she called, "And why do you dare come here? The color of death is not yet on you."

"I am Hermod, son of Odin," said the young warrior. "I seek Balder, who was taken from us in the field of Idavollr."

"He has already ridden over the bridge," said Modgudur. "But you cannot. Go north, to Helheim."

So Hermod rode on until he reached the gates of the terrible kingdom, where Garm tore at him with bloody jaws. But Sleipnir cleared the towering black gates with one great leap, and they began to travel through the regions of the dead. At last Hermod saw Balder, all light gone out of him, sitting silently with Nanna and the other spirits, and he went to the goddess Hel, fell on his knees and begged her to release him.

"You say all things on earth love Balder," she said. "Then let all things weep for him. Let their tears make a river to carry him out of Helheim into the light of day again. But I tell you this: if any living thing refuses, Balder stays mine, and will never return to Asgard."

With hope in his heart Hermod turned Sleipnir's head to the east and rode forth again. At last he reached Asgard and delivered his message to Odin.

Then all creation wept for Balder, the birds of the air and the sea creatures, the trees and the grass, the very stones themselves. Even the giants wept, in their lonely fastnesses of snow and ice. And the goddess heard in Helheim, but still she would not release him. "One creature witholds her tears," she said, "and so it cannot be."

This creature was Thaukt the Old, an ancient giantess.

When the gods asked her to weep for Balder she gave a bitter, twisted laugh. "I will weep dry tears for him," she screamed in fury. "He did nothing for me when he was alive. Let Hel keep what is hers!"

Now Odin knew that the giantess was really Loki the Jealous. "He has taken away Balder," he said, "he has taken away the Shining One. Now he must be bound in chains until the day of Ragnarok when, in the Twilight of the Gods, all chains shall be broken." But even as they hunted for him Loki had changed himself into a salmon and had hidden in a deep pool by a waterfall, where he was certain that the gods would never find him. But at last, after much searching, they saw him in the pool, and weaving a great net, they trapped him in its meshes. He twisted and leaped about and had almost broken free when Thor caught him by the tail and held him fast, so that to this day salmon have the narrowest of tails.

Then, when he was his old shape again, they bound him fast to sharp rocks in a cave underneath the earth, where he remained until the coming of Ragnarok.

Balder also remained under the earth, in Helheim, with the sad, pale gods. But up above, the creatures still weep for him; for the Shining One even the stones cry out. And when the morning sun rises, warming the icy rocks, they too weep tears.

PERSEPHONE

A Greek Myth

At the beginning of time, when the gods defeated the giants, the world was divided into three by the casting of lots. Zeus won the sky, and his brother Poseidon the sea. The underworld was left to Hades. He was a brooding, lonely god, and he begged Zeus to give him a wife from the land above. He had fallen in love with Persephone, the daughter of Demeter.

Demeter was the most powerful of all the goddesses; she ruled over every living thing on earth, and without her nothing would grow. Zeus knew that she would never agree to let her daughter marry Hades, and he feared her anger if he dared ask such a question. But the king of the underworld was determined that Persephone would be his wife, and he decided to carry her off by force.

For many days he waited and watched. Then, one morning, he heard that she was out in the meadows on the slopes of Mount Etna, picking flowers with the Daughters of Ocean. These nymphs were very beautiful, but none of them so beautiful as the radiant Persephone. She outshone them as day outshines night.

Zeus had conspired with Hades to help him trap her, and now, at her feet, she saw a most marvelous plant appear from nowhere. It was a white narcissus with a hundred flowers growing from its root, a thing so lovely and so fragrant that not only mortals but the gods themselves wondered at it.

Persephone bent down to pick the flower. But, as her fingers closed on it, the mountain split open with a terrible roaring noise, and from the depths came Hades riding on his black chariot, pulled by huge black horses. With a cry of triumph he swept the terrified Persephone up into the chariot and galloped away, down to the underworld.

Two others knew about this cruel thing. One was old Hecate, the witch goddess, who had heard how the girl cried out in terror. The other was Helios, god of the sun, who had seen the enormous black chariot rise up from the gash in the earth, and the greedy fingers of Hades, snatching the girl away. But he was driving his sun horses across the sky and could not cease in his labors until the day was done.

Demeter also heard the echo of her daughter's voice, from far away, on Mount Parthenia, and she set off at once to find her, wandering over the earth, not stopping to eat or drink, and taking no rest. On the ninth day she met old Hecate, who told her she had heard the girl cry out on Mount Etna. Then she met Helios, who confessed that he too knew what had happened, and that Zeus had plotted to help his brother Hades by setting the white flower at Persephone's feet.

When she heard this, Demeter's grief turned to rage. She left Mount Olympus, where the gods lived, disguised herself as an old woman, and went to Eleusis, where she built a temple and spent long days there, mourning and weeping for her lost daughter.

And she turned her back upon the earth and all that she must do there to make things grow. For a whole year the land sent up no shoots, and cattle pulled plows across the fields in vain. The white barley seed fell useless from the sower's hand, and rotted where it lay.

People began to starve, and in alarm Zeus sent Iris, the

goddess of the rainbow, down to earth to plead for mercy from the goddess of grain. But Demeter refused to listen to her, nor would she listen to Zeus's other messengers. Day after day she sat alone in her temple at Eleusis, vowing that she would never return to Olympus, or allow any green thing to grow upon earth until Persephone was restored to her.

At last Zeus sent his own son, Hermes, to plead with the god of the underworld. He knew the way well, for it was his task to lead the dead from earth down to hell. Sad-faced, he stood before Hades' throne, having taken off his winged sandals and set aside the gold rod with which he pointed the way. And the tragic Persephone, so small on her great black throne, listened in silence as he pleaded with her husband.

"Great Hades," he said. "Upon earth people are dying because Demeter has put a curse on all her crops. Release Persephone, I beg you. If you do not, Zeus will soon have no subjects to rule over. This kingdom too will die, for the world will be empty." And the tears ran down his face.

Hades thought for a moment, then rose, and put his queen's hand into that of Hermes. "Go," he said, "since Zeus commands it. But do not forget me, Persephone. I have been kind to you. Remember too that all the souls here remain your subjects, wherever you may be." And he turned away sadly, into his dark kingdom.

So they returned joyously to earth, and Persephone was restored to her mother's arms. But then the goddess drew back, for the stain of a fruit was upon the girl's mouth. "Did you eat in the underworld?" she asked fearfully.

"Only a few seeds from a pomegranate," answered the innocent Persephone. Then Demeter knew that Hades had tricked them, for whoever eats food in the kingdom of the dead cannot ever escape from it.

So Zeus made a pact with his brother, and for six months of the year Persephone has to live with her dark king, under the earth. In those short, hard days, nothing grows upon earth. Demeter mourns for her daughter in a dress of frost and snow.

When the girl is restored to her, Demeter's heart grows light again. Spring comes, and blossom. After this the summer opens out in glory, and then the rich harvest appears. Only when Hades claims his queen again does the year begin to sicken and die.

Then people remember Persephone, and they remember too that the dark and cold are only for a season and that the winter woods always contain the promise of a new spring.

BEDD GELERT

A Welsh Legend

There was once a great prince named Llewellyn and he had a beloved only son. His wife had died when the baby was born, making the child doubly precious to him. Although Llewellyn was rich, with many servants, he entrusted the care of his infant son to an old dog called Gelert. This faithful creature had accompanied the prince on many journeys and had fought by his side in many battles. No human was braver, or more true, and he loved Llewellyn's baby son like a mother.

One day, when the child was fast asleep in his cradle, Llewellyn heard horns outside, hallooing, and the baying of hounds. "I must join the hunt," he said, "they are riding over my lands." And he began to prepare himself. Gelert got up, wagged his tail hopefully, and looked at his master. "No, Gelert," said the prince. "Your place is by the cradle. Guard it till I return; guard it with your life."

So the obedient dog trotted to the baby's side and lay down, putting his nose in his paws. Llewellyn patted him and set off for the hunt, knowing that he could not have left the little prince in safer keeping than with old Gelert.

But not many hours had passed before the dog scented danger. Something was pushing the door open, something that breathed hard and fast, something with a foul, rank smell. Gelert got up, every hair on his back bristling, and began to creep cautiously across the floor. A wolf was standing there. It was huge, and it towered over the dog, yet it was scraggy and thin. It had been a hard winter and meat was scarce; the wolf was desperately hungry. A succulent human child would make a good meal. Smelling the sweet young flesh, the wolf made a sudden leap toward the cradle.

Gelert threw himself on the slavering animal, tearing at it with his claws and dragging it away from the little prince, trying to force it back through the door so that he could finish it off in the open air, away from the slumbering child.

But the wolf was maddened by hunger and by the scent of the baby. It bit great lumps out of Gelert's neck and side, and with the old dog still hanging onto it, forced its way back across the room until it was within a hair's breadth of the cradle.

Then Gelert too went mad, and the two creatures rolled over and over on the floor, each trying to get at the other's throat and eyes in a wild, yelping fury of teeth, hair, and skin. Miraculously, through all this, the tiny baby slept on, never stirring when, in the frenzied fight, the rocking cradle overturned, tipping him out onto the cold flagstones, or when warm blood spattered his face, running down the walls and soaking into the embroidered coverlet.

With one last mighty effort, and strengthened by the dread of his master's returning home to find the corpse of his beloved son, Gelert bared his teeth yet again, sinking them deep into the wolf's scrawny neck. With a terrible roar of pain, the beast twisted to get free, crept defeated into a corner, and died.

At once Gelert went to the overturned cradle, took the bloodstained coverlet into his mouth and dragged it over the baby, who still slept on. Then he lay down beside him and slept too.

When Llewellyn returned from the hunt, the exhausted dog got wearily to his feet and limped over to greet him, wagging his tail. But the prince had eyes for nothing but the overturned cradle, the stained coverlet and the blood on the walls. Even the child's face was bloody.

He did not see the dead wolf heaped in the corner. All he could see was that, in some fit of madness, Gelert had killed his only son. Drawing his sword, he raised it high above the dog's head, and even as Gelert jumped up wanting to play, and wanting praise for what he had done, plunged it deep into his heart, and killed him.

At that moment the baby started crying. Gelert's puzzled little bark had woken him at last and now he was hungry and cold, not able to understand why he was lying on a chilly floor, only half-covered with sticky, damp clothes.

Llewellyn's sword clattered onto the flagstones as he saw in horror the dead wolf lying in the corner, saw the lumps of hair, the blood, all the evidence of a terrible fight. And he wept aloud, paying no heed to the squalling baby but gathering the body of Gelert into his arms, as if he too were his child. He was never to forget that day, and it was many, many years before the awful memory of it began to dim in his mind.

All this was centuries ago, but today, in the graveyard of the village of Bedd Gelert, you will find an old mossy stone carved with the words "To the Memory of a Brave Dog." Underneath is written this story. It is the resting place of Gelert, a grave put there by a sorrowing prince, for his best friend.

THE HARE IN THE MOON

A Legend from India

Once upon a time there were four good friends: an otter, a monkey, a jackal, and a hare. Every night they met in the forest to talk about the day that had passed and to discuss what they might best do with their lives. The hare was the wisest of the four, and he was always telling the others stories about the deeds of men, of how good they could be, and how kind to their friends in need.

"We should try to be like that," he said one evening, settling himself down to sleep. Then he looked up at the moon. "It's the middle of the month," he told his friends. "Tomorrow men will neither eat nor drink. Instead, they will give money and food to any holy man or beggar who asks them. Why don't we do the same?"

The friends agreed that this was an excellent idea, and early next day they got up and went their separate ways.

The otter bounded down to the river and caught a fine fish for his breakfast. Then, remembering that he'd taken a vow

not to eat for the whole day, he carried the fish home so that he could eat it the minute the sun went down. Then he curled up and went to sleep.

The jackal went to town and scavenged around all the garbage dumps until he found a hunk of meat. Like the otter, he carried it back home and hid it, then he too went to sleep, and the monkey did the same with the huge bunch of mangoes he'd picked. All three snoozed the day away, and dreamed about the marvelous suppers they were going to have when darkness fell. They felt less hungry that way, and besides, if they were fast asleep, people couldn't come pestering them for money.

When the hare woke up he scampered about over the dewy grass. It smelled very good, and his mouth watered, but he knew he mustn't eat a single blade of it, because he was fasting, like the humans.

As he stared longingly at the grass he began to worry. "I have no money or food to give to the holy men or the beggars," he said to himself, "and they can't eat grass." Then a terrible thought struck him. He remembered that

human beings like eating the flesh of the hare. "I have made my vow," he said bravely, "and I must give food to anyone who asks. I am good to eat, so I must give myself."

The god Sakka had been listening, hidden in a passing cloud. "I will put him to the test," he said. "Few men would give up their lives for others, so how could a mere hare do such a thing?" Changing himself into the shape of an old man, he came down from his cloud and, toward evening, drew near to the hare's meadow. "Can you give me anything to eat?" he asked the creature. "I have had nothing all day."

"I have only myself," answered the hare. "Could you make a meal of me?"

"Yes, indeed," the god said, "but this is a holy day and I am forbidden to kill animals with my own hands."

"Heap sticks together, and make a fire," suggested the hare. "I will jump into it, and you can eat roast meat."

Sakka was astonished at the hare's bravery, yet still he had to test him further, so he uttered some words of power and a great fire sprang up. At

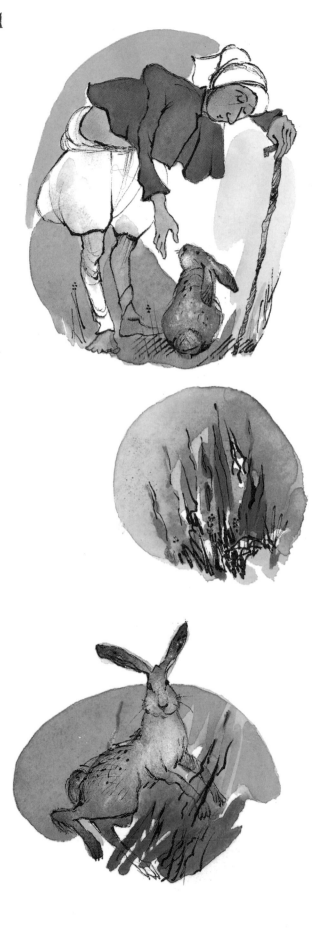

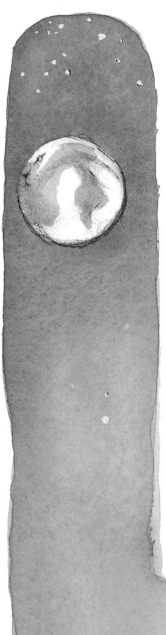

once, true to his word, the hare leaped into the middle of it. Although the flames swirled all around him, not a hair of his silken coat was touched.

"Old man," he called out in wonder, "I am in the fire, as you commanded, and yet I do not burn."

Then the god appeared before the hare in all his glory, caused the fire to die away, and said, "I am Sakka, the Almighty. I heard your vow and I came to put you to the test. Such courage and love as this is beyond anything the gods have ever seen before. Your story must be made known throughout the world, to all men, for ever."

Stretching out his hand, the god drew from the nearby mountain some magic thing which ran deep inside its rocky veins, and threw it at the rising moon. At once, the shape of the hare appeared in it, black against the silver brightness.

"Take your reward, little creature," said the god. "You shall live for ever on the moon's face, and when they look at you, people will remember an ancient truth: "Give to others, and the gods will give to you.""

THE UNICORN

A Celtic Legend

Long ago, in the days of King Arthur and his knights, there lived a girl named Rhiannon. Her father had been thrown into prison by the cruel Sir Brangwyn, who said he'd been stealing deer from the forest. This was a lie. Her father was one of the most honorable men in the village, and that was why Sir Brangwyn had gotten rid of him. With men like Rhiannon's father around, the great lord wouldn't have dared to cheat and lie, and to demand such high taxes. He'd been put in prison to keep his mouth shut.

Rhiannon's mother had to work in the castle kitchen to pay for the miserable scraps of food her husband ate. So, when this story begins, poor Rhiannon had neither father nor mother. People called her "Sir Brangwyn's orphan," and how she hated him for taking away her innocent parents!

She had to work too, even though she was only nine years old. Her job was to hunt for truffles in the forest. Sir Brangwyn was a huge fat man, who loved his food, and he loved the delicately flavored truffles best of all — those sweet, fleshy things that grow on the roots of trees. But they

were hard to find, and Rhiannon often searched all day and uncovered only a handful.

Next to feasting, Sir Brangwyn loved the hunt, and often, while Rhiannon was out in the woods, he and his knights would come crashing through the trees after the deer. People said there were still ancient beasts in Sir Brangwyn's woods, unicorns and dragons, and basilisks, whose gaze could turn you to stone. But Rhiannon had never seen anything like that.

A year to the day after her father had been imprisoned, she went into the woods with her basket to hunt for truffles. That night she was followed back to the edge of the trees by a beautiful little horse, pure white, only a foal, with a silky mane and tail.

The people of the village tried to catch it, thinking that perhaps Sir Brangwyn would take it instead of their tax money. But it darted away and vanished into the forest, leaving Rhiannon alone. However, her basket was heaped with precious truffles. "It showed me where to dig," she said shyly.

Next morning the villagers set off to find the little white horse for themselves. If it could lead them to a horde of truffles their problems with greedy Sir Brangwyn would be over. They could use the truffles to pay their taxes, and have money left for their own needs. But though they waited all day, there was no sign of Rhiannon's horse. Only when they had gone home did it come to her, shimmering through the trees, and again, truffles filled her basket.

Day after day the same thing happened. Sir Brangwyn's clerk, who was a monk and a clever man, questioned one of the castle servants about Rhiannon's mysterious little white horse, and one night the servant spied on her in the forest. "It is just as the girl has told us," he said. "The creature runs around in the trees, and where it stops and paws at the ground, she digs, and finds truffles. When her basket is full, it puts its head in her lap, and she sings to it. It's a fine little beast," he went on, "there's just one thing. . ."

"*Yes*?" said the monk keenly, for he had guessed the truth. "There's a lump between its eyes, as if, as it. . ."

"As if a horn were coming," murmured the monk. And he

knew then that Rhiannon's white horse was a magic creature, a unicorn.

The minute the news reached Sir Brangwyn he called together his best huntsmen. There had been no unicorn in the woods for hundreds of years. It would be a prize indeed. The village turned out to help him, setting traps and going into the forest to watch for the little white horse, but nothing did any good. Day after day they all trailed home disappointed. The unicorn had vanished.

Sir Brangwyn began to grow impatient. Then the old monk, his clerk, told him what was needed. The surest way to catch a unicorn was to send a young girl alone into the woods, to lure it into a clearing. There she could sing to it, until it fell asleep. It would not see the huntsmen coming, and the prize would be theirs.

So poor Rhiannon was dragged before Sir Brangwyn and told what she must do. Her tears and protests did no good at all; he said he would kill her parents if she didn't help him. What could she do but go with the royal huntsmen into the forest and watch, sick at heart, while they heaped up a great bank of brushwood, behind which they and their horses could hide, until the unicorn came?

All night they kept watch, with Sir Brangwyn the most eager-eyed of all, waiting behind the heaped-up branches on his huge black horse, a great spear in his hand. At last the unicorn came, like moonlight painting the dark trees, looking nervously this way and that, pawing the ground. Then, scenting its friend, Rhiannon, it bounded up to her, kissed her on the forehead, and lay down, with its head in her lap.

But this time she did not sing, and it looked up, puzzled, into her face. At the same moment Sir Brangwyn came thundering through the trees with a cry of triumph, his spear flashing and the blood running down the sides of his great black charger, as he spurred it cruelly on. Rhiannon leaped up, flung her arms around the unicorn's neck, and dragged it into the forest, and Sir Brangwyn roared after them, the blade of his spear poised for one awful thrust.

Creeping out from behind the brushwood, the huntsmen and the villagers waited for their lord to return with his prize. But nobody came. All they heard was a crashing of hooves and a great whinnying noise, a long cry of pain, then silence.

Hidden in the shadows, Rhiannon watched as they hunted for Sir Brangwyn. In the end, after many hours, they found him lying dead in the forest. There was no sign of his horse, or of his murderous spear. But something had pierced him to the heart, and he lay staring glassily into the trees in a great pool of blood.

Sir Ivor, son of the wicked Sir Brangwyn, was as kind as his father had been cruel. He emptied the castle dungeons; Rhiannon's parents were restored to her and took her home.

What she had seen that day in the forest remained her secret forever. All they knew of it were four little words, whispered sleepily one night, as she fell asleep in her mother's arms.

"Unicorns have parents, too."

THE WILLOW PATTERN STORY

A Chinese Legend

Koong-se was the daughter of a rich old man named T'so Ling. She was in love with Chang, a humble scribe who came every day to her father's house to write letters for him in his beautiful script. Chang was a poet too, and he wrote poems to Koong-se which she had to read in secret. There was no chance that they would ever marry; her father was too proud. Then Koong-se's maid had an idea. Why didn't the lovers meet in the little summer-house which was tucked away in a corner of T'so Ling's enormous garden? "Perfect," said Koong-se, when she saw it, and they started to meet there every day. Chang gave her his poems, and she gave him some blue beads.

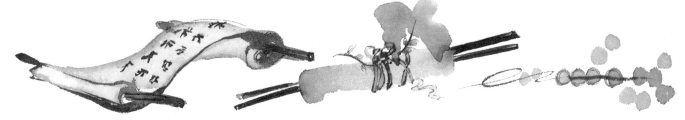

But old T'so Ling, who was always snooping around, found them there and flew into a great rage. Chang was sent away and told that he would be put to death if ever he returned. Koong-se's little maid was sent away too; in her place came a witchy old woman with a hard, cruel face. She guarded Koong-se day and night.

Then T'so Ling had a huge fence built all around the house and a special terrace for his daughter to walk on, which jutted out into the garden. She could see the flowers and the river, with its great willow tree weeping into the water, but she couldn't reach them anymore. And there was no chance of Chang's rowing up the river to snatch a glimpse of her either. T'so Ling's great hall, where he spent his day counting his money, had windows that looked down into the garden.

One day T'so Ling told his daughter that she was to marry a great lord, a Ta-jin of enormous wealth. He too was old, and greedy. "How lucky you are!" croaked the old witch woman who guarded her, but Koong-se wept. She knew she would be married to the hideous Ta-jin when the peach tree outside her window came into bloom. How she envied the birds their freedom as they flew in and out of its branches.

Chang, hearing about the marriage, wrote a poem and sent it down the river in a coconut shell. "If you become his wife," it said, "my poor heart will break."

"Then save me," begged Koong-se, sending back her message in the bobbing coconut shell.

But the days passed and no word came from Chang. The peach tree was nearly in blossom, and in T'so Ling's house the marriage feast was being prepared. Koong-se was not to meet her husband till the wedding morning, but the night before, the two old men got very drunk, and this was Chang's great chance. Stealing through the garden and into the house, he crept past the snoring old witch woman. Then he put on a coat belonging to one of T'so Ling's drunken servants, freed Koong-se from her chamber, and crept away with her into the shadow of the willow tree. With her she brought her distaff, the special rod on which she wound her yarn. From now on they would be poor, and she would have to earn her living. Chang carried a box of jewels which the Ta-jin had brought as a wedding gift.

Something woke the sleeping T'so Ling, and finding his daughter's room empty, he rushed out into the garden. There were the lovers, hurrying across the bridge. With terrible cries he pursued them, but they were young, and he was a fat, drunk old man. By the time he reached the bridge they had disappeared, and although his servants hunted high and low for them, all trace of Koong-se and her beloved Chang had vanished.

For weeks T'so Ling's servants looked for them, but in vain. In fact, they were close at hand, living in a tiny gardener's cottage not very far from the house. They had

been married there in secret, and they were very happy, except that they could venture outside only after dark. By day the place swarmed with T'so Ling's servants, and the Ta-jin had threatened to kill the young couple if they ever showed their faces again. He was a proud man, and he had been cheated of a beautiful wife, not to mention his jewels.

In the end Koong-se's father ordered soldiers to join the hunt for the vanished lovers. Someone had told him they might be hiding in the gardener's cottage. Up they marched to the door and banged so hard the little house shook. The gardener's wife, who was a clever woman, kept them talking and gave them food and drink while Chang and his bride made their escape. The river flowed behind the house, and although it was swollen with all the winter's rain, Chang plunged in and managed to swim to the opposite shore, where a little boat was moored. In this they made their escape, and when the soldiers at last forced their way into the cottage, they found only footprints on the floor, and an open window through which the cold night air was blowing.

After a long and dangerous journey on the great Yangtze Kiang River, Chang and Koong-se found a small deserted

island, where they set up house. Koong-se spun yarn, Chang sold the Ta-jin's jewels to buy what they needed, and they lived there together in perfect contentment for many years. Chang planted seeds, and his crops grew tall. He began to write poems again, and books about the simple country life which had brought them such happiness.

But it was these very books that brought an end to everything, for they became famous, and the Ta-jin, that rich old man who had planned to marry Koong-se, read them and vowed even now to take his revenge. Gathering soldiers together, he gave them cruel commands, and in no time at all they had found the secret island where Chang, the famous farmer and poet, lived.

Within minutes Chang lay dead, a sword through his heart, and poor Koong-se, unable to carry on living without her beloved Chang at her side, ran into the house and set fire to it.

But that isn't the end of the Willow Pattern Story, for the gods, moved to pity by the great love between Chang and Koong-se, turned them into two doves. And now they fly for ever above the willow tree by the bridge, cooing softly to each other as the peach tree blossoms.

KING MIDAS

A Greek Myth

Midas was the King of Macedonia, and he was very rich. With his money he bought beautiful things, filling his palace with treasures and his garden with the most marvelous flowers and plants. He liked to walk there early in the morning, plotting how to get richer still, so that he might buy even more lovely things to fill his bulging money chests.

His greatest treasure of all, however, was his daughter. She cared nothing for her father's wealth. What she liked best was to play in the palace gardens and to pick bunches of flowers. Roses were her favorite, and each morning she would pick the most perfect bloom she could find and put it on Midas's breakfast plate.

One morning, as he was taking his usual early walk, he heard a curious snoring noise coming from under a hedge. Creeping up, he gave it a shake, then watched to see what would happen. First a little hairy leg appeared, then another, then a tail.

"*Humph!*" said the king to himself. "A goat's gotten into my garden, the dirty, smelly thing. I must make sure there are no holes in the fences, otherwise all my precious plants will be eaten. Now come on, you!" And he kicked at it.

The thing under the hedge stopped snoring, then, with a splutter and a sneeze, it slowly uncurled itself and stared up at the great king in terror. It wasn't a goat at all, it was a

satyr: half animal, half man. The creature's name was Silenus and Midas knew him very well.

"What are you doing here?" the King said, tugging him by the beard, "crushing my flowers with that great fat belly of yours? Why aren't you with your master?"

Now the lord of the satyrs was Dionysus, the god of wine, and old Silenus had obviously been drinking at one of his parties. His face was as red as a holly berry, and Midas's neat flower beds were littered with empty wine skins. "Pl...please, sir," he stammered, "we were all coming back from a feast and the others went home without me. I'm an old man, and they were going too fast. I got lost. Oh please, great sir, forgive me. . . ." And a big tear rolled down his cheek. He was frightened of Midas. Everyone knew what a greedy man he was, and how he'd stop at nothing to get what he wanted, especially if there was money in it. Gold was his god.

But to Silenus's surprise the king's face softened. "On your feet, you old rogue," he said with a smile. "It's too lovely a morning for a quarrel, and I want my breakfast. Come on, you'd better have some too."

The satyr stayed in the royal palace for five days and nights. The king had very few friends — he was too proud, and too greedy — so he rather enjoyed listening to the old man's stories, watching him eat huge meals and drink the very best wine in the palace cellars. Every evening the gardeners brought garlands of roses and twined them around his neck. Old Silenus felt like a king himself. He couldn't thank Midas enough.

Neither could his master, Dionysus. When at last he came to take the old man home, he offered Midas a gift. "In return for your great kindness to my servant," he said, "I will grant you any wish you care to name."

Midas's eyes gleamed. He didn't need time to think up an answer. "My lord," he said, "grant that whatever I touch shall be turned into gold." That way he would surely win his heart's desire, to be the richest man in the world.

"It shall be so," said Dionysus and, taking Silenus by the arm, he went away to his own kingdom. But his step was slow, Midas noticed, and his face troubled.

Next day the king woke up very early. He couldn't wait to see if Dionysus had kept his promise. But the minute he put on his kingly robes he knew it was so, for everything he touched, the goblet by his bed, the dish of grapes, the basin of water, all became solid and hard under his fingers, and glittered marvelously in the morning light. It was true. *He had the golden touch!*

He hurried out to his beloved rose garden, stumbling a little because his golden tunic and sandals were now so very heavy, and began to walk around his flower beds. The air was full of birdsong and sweet with the smell of the roses. Everywhere the bees hummed busily. Midas stretched out his hand and touched the nearest flower. A single rose could be worth a fortune, now he had the golden touch. Suddenly a kind of madness seized him and he went up and down the rose garden turning all the fragile pink and yellow and creamy blossoms to pure gold. When he had finished he turned back toward his palace. He was quite hungry now, and he needed a good breakfast inside him before he set about making the biggest fortune the world had ever known. He was much too excited to notice that the heavy gold heads of the roses had crashed down to the earth, that all the birds had stopped singing, and that the bees had gone away.

Midas ordered a grand breakfast for himself, and while he

was waiting for it he turned his plate and his goblet, his table and his chair into gold. These alone must have been worth many fortunes, but greedy Midas wanted more. The minute he had food inside him he would begin in earnest. . . . But what was this? The delicious warm bread his servant had set before him turned into a hard, cold lump halfway to his mouth; the peaches, figs, and grapes became solid as soon as he tried to eat them; the honey gleamed gold in its solid gold comb and the pitcher of milk broke into pieces, too frail for the weight of gold inside it. Oh yes, King Midas was indeed rich now but he was hungry too, and, deep inside him, a little worm of panic had began to wriggle and gnaw. The golden touch was a marvelous gift, but it was a dangerous one. From now on he would have to be very careful before he touched things. Perhaps he would call a servant to come and put the food into his mouth.

There he sat at his solid gold table, in his solid gold chair, unable to eat the solid gold bread and fruit or to drink the solid gold milk. It was very silent. No birdsong came through the windows, no hum of bees, and the fragrance of the roses had gone forever. They were all gold now, lying on the earth on their broken solid gold stems. Even his daughter was unhappy today, for instead of her usual laughter, he could hear a sobbing noise, floating through the corridors of the great palace.

"Father," she wept, as she ran up to him, "something terrible has happened. The roses have a disease, they have no colors any more, and no smell, they're just lying all over the garden and the bushes are all broken down. I went out to pick one for you but I. . ."

"*Stop!*" A sudden fear had come upon Midas and he stretched out his hands. "Don't come any closer, I beg you." The only living, breathing thing in his hateful, dead kingdom of gold was this child with her raven-black hair; she was more precious to him than life. "*Stop!*" he cried again, but she took no notice. She was young, her mother was dead, and some awful spell had come upon her rose garden. She needed her father's arms around her, so she tried to climb upon his knee.

Their fingers touched, the father's and the child's, and in that moment she turned into a little gold statue, her arms forever stretched out, seeking comfort, her hair blown around her face, and the tears halfway down her cheeks. Midas, seeing them, wept too.

The days passed, and nobody came near him. Whispers had gone around the royal household that the king was cursed, and even greedier than they had supposed. Had he not turned everything to gold, even his own daughter?

There sat Midas in his great gold chair, his gold bread and milk untouched before him, weeping over his dead, gold daughter and wishing with all his heart that he had not been so foolish, or so greedy. He remembered the sorrow in Dionysus's face, when he had first asked for the golden touch. Now he understood.

And suddenly the god was standing before him. "What is the matter, Midas?" he said. "Did I not grant you your heart's desire, and are you not the richest man in the world?"

"Yes, yes, my lord, but I am also the unhappiest, for I have lost my daughter, and all this is nothing to me without her. Take away the golden touch, I beg you. Let all be as before and I shall never again seek riches beyond the dreams of man."

"Do you promise?" said Dionysus gravely. He was not at all sure the king could be trusted, even now.

"By all the gods, I swear," he answered, and seeing the lifeless statue of his daughter, he cried aloud, begging Dionysus to have mercy on him.

"Very well. You must go and wash in the waters of the River Paktolos. Let its waters flow over you, and all will be well. Set off at once, for it's a long journey." And the god disappeared.

It took Midas weeks to reach the river, for he was faint from lack of food, and he could hardly drag himself along the ground. But at last, after many days, when he thought he could go no farther, he saw the blue gleam of water in the distance. But he needed strength to reach it. Stretching up, he plucked fruit from an overhanging branch. Surely Dionysus had already freed him from the curse? But no, the fruit turned cold and hard in his mouth, as before. Spitting it out, he crawled inch by agonizing inch to the river's edge, threw himself in and bathed his burning limbs in its soothing waters, washing away the terrible golden touch. To this day people go looking for gold in the River Paktolos.

When he was back on shore Midas touched the stones on

the brink with trembling fingers. What if Dionysus had cheated him? What if the golden touch remained? But no, the pebbles shone white and brown and speckled, like eggs. He was free, free from the curse of gold, for ever and ever. Stopping only to quench his thirst, he set off for home, laughing aloud in his joy. All he wanted was to enfold his daughter in his arms again.

And there she was, waiting for him in the rose garden. Inside the palace his servants stood ready with fresh robes, and with food and drink. All was as it had been before, except that his daughter's dark hair was now the palest gold. That was Dionysus's doing. It was to remind Midas of his foolishness, and to show him that the love of a child matters far more than the love of gold.

THE WISHING FISH

A Tale from Russia

There was once a poor old man who went down to the sea-shore to try to catch some fish. He was all skin and bone, and his wife was no better. Catches had been getting poorer and poorer, and there was no food left for them to eat. The old man toiled all day but caught nothing in his net.

Then, just as he was about to give up and return home empty-handed, he felt his net grow heavy. Excited, he started to haul it in toward the shore, but it was very hard work, it now weighed so much. There must be dozens of fish inside it, he thought, at last I'm in luck! But when the net came out of the water he had a great surprise. All that was in it was one tiny little fish, flopping about on the sand.

"Throw me back into the sea, I beg you," it gasped. "I am no ordinary fish, I promise." And this was true, for the fish was made of pure gold, and the evening sun glittered on its fins and tail as it squirmed about helplessly.

The old man could have sold the golden fish and lived in comfort for the rest of his life, but he had a kind heart. Gently he picked it up and threw it back into the sea, then, heaving his net over his shoulder, he trudged off up the beach.

"Come back, old man!" called a voice. There, standing on its tail in the sea, was the little gold fish. "You have saved my life," it said, "and now I have power to give you whatever you want. What can I do for you? Only name it, and it shall be done."

The old man had had nothing to eat that day, and hunger was gnawing at his insides. "Bread," he said, "do you think we could have some bread, me and my poor wife?"

"Of course," said the fish. "Go home. There is plenty of bread there. It will feed you both for a week."

And it was true. The old man's broken-down fishing hut was bulging with loaves of bread, with buns and with delicious gooey cakes, and in the middle of it all, sat his wife, stuffing food into her mouth just as fast as she could. The old man took a piece of bread, sat down and began to eat. "I found a little gold fish down on the beach," he explained, "just a little one, you understand, nothing you could have made a meal of, and because I threw it back in the sea it said it would give me anything I cared to name. So I thought we'd better have some food right away."

When she heard this the old woman's mouth dropped open. "You fool!" she shrieked, giving him a kick. "I want more than that! Your precious fish can fix up this hut, to begin with — it's a disgrace. Go back and tell him so, this minute!"

The poor old man scuttled back to the beach and called to the golden fish. "Little fish, little fish," he cried, and immediately the golden fish popped out of the waves and stood on its tail.

"Forgive me, but my wife's still not happy. Could we possibly have a few sticks of furniture for our hut, and some new thatch, perhaps? The roof leaks badly."

"All shall be as you wish," said the fish. "Go home."

When he reached his hut the old man thought he must be dreaming. It was now a pretty little cottage with new thatch as yellow as butter, roses around the door, and inside, rooms full of pretty furniture and a soft feather bed on which his wife lay, snoring loudly. "At last she is happy," he said to himself, creeping away to mend his nets. But he was wrong, for within a few weeks she was nagging at him again.

"This cottage is too small for us," she said, "and I need someone to do the gardening. Go back to that fish of yours and tell him I want to live in the Lord Mayor's house. In fact, I want to be the Lord Mayor. I'm tired of doing housework." So the old man went back to the fish and called out "Little fish, little fish. I'm so sorry but my wife still isn't happy. Now she wants to be the Lord Mayor, and to live in his great house in town."

"Go home," said the fish. "She has what she wants." And when the old man reached his cottage he found it had vanished away. There instead was the Lord Mayor's house, with its rows of gleaming windows and its great sweeps

of green lawn. "Be off with you!" she yelled at her husband, who was still in his rags, and she climbed into her carriage and rode off into town to do some shopping.

But she wasn't content for very long. A few weeks later she sent for her husband once more. "It's all very well being the Lord Mayor," she said, "but it's boring, stuck in this dirty little town. I think I want to be queen. Go on, find that fish of yours and get it fixed up."

The old man trembled. "Wife," he began gently, "can you not be happy with what you have, first a lovely cottage and now the Lord Mayor's house?"

"I WANT TO BE QUEEN!" she screeched yet again, "I WANT TO BE. . ." But the old man didn't wait to hear any more. He rushed off to the seashore to find the golden fish.

When it heard what the old woman wanted this time it gave a little sigh. Nevertheless, it stood on its tail obligingly and sent him away with the promise that his wife should have all she asked.

When he reached town again the Lord Mayor's house had been replaced by a shimmering golden palace. You couldn't see it for all the servants, rushing here and there, with dishes of food and armfuls of new clothes, all sent for by the very ugly new queen who sat in the middle on a great golden throne, barking orders at everybody. The old man was ashamed. He crept away into the palace kitchens and sat with the servants, dreading the day when his wife would send for him again.

Sure enough, a few weeks later, the Lord Chancellor dragged him before his wife's throne. "*You*," she said, to the trembling old man, "get back to that fish and quickly, or I'll have your head chopped off. Tell him I'm sick of being queen. It's time I was ruler of the world. That's it, I'll be Empress of the Seven Seas. Nobody's more powerful than that."

The old man didn't argue; he was frightened of what his wife might do to him. She seemed to be going mad. Sick at heart he dragged himself down to the beach again and whispered his request in such a little voice that the fish couldn't hear him. "Speak louder," it called above the crashing of the waves.

"I hate to ask you," the old man mumbled, "but she wants to be Empress of the Seven Seas now. She says being queen's not good enough."

"Very well," said the fish, "she is Empress. But tell her this. There is only one wish left. I advise her to think very carefully indeed before sending you here again."

The old man thanked the golden fish, turned away, and plodded back to the palace. It took him a long time because it was now perched on top of a mountain made of glass. The palace was glass too, and ten times bigger than the other

one and with hundreds more servants. There sat his wife, a golden telescope held up to her eye, surveying the seven seas and purring loudly, like an enormous cat.

"I have a message from the fish," the old man said boldly. "There is only one wish left, and he wants you to think very carefully before you send me back again."

The old woman dropped the telescope, and the purring stopped abruptly. "Very well," she said, "you can go back right away."

"What do you want this time?" her husband said wearily. "Surely nothing is better than being Empress of the Seven Seas."

"I want to be God," she said.

With great terror in his heart the old man stood once again on the seashore. "Little fish, little fish," he called, hoping that the creature would not hear him this time. But a gold fin sliced through the water, and there it was as before. "She wants to be God," he whispered.

"Go home, old man," said the fish, "that is not mine to give." So the old man went away, and when he got home he found the great glass palace had been replaced by his smelly old fishing hut, with his wife sitting outside it, stirring a smoky fire.

THE GIANTS WHO COULDN'T SWIM

An Irish Legend

This is the story of two giants. One lived all alone in a cave in Scotland, on a rocky island called Staffa. He was named Bennadonner. The other lived with his wife in a snug stone house on the wild north coast of Antrim, in Ireland. His name was Finn MacCool.

Both the giants had magic powers. Finn had a Thumb of Knowledge which told him what to do when he got into a muddle. He simply sucked it like a baby, and the right answer came to him. Bennadonner had a Magic Finger which let him see into the future, and which warned him when trouble was brewing.

When Finn MacCool was young he'd fallen in love with a beautiful giantess who lived next door to Bennadonner, on his rocky island. The problem was that he couldn't swim, so he chopped down a forest and built a huge boat so that he could sail across the Irish Sea. But it sank the minute he set foot in it, for he weighed as much as a small mountain.

For a while he couldn't think how to cross the water. Then he had an idea. He gathered together some huge pieces of rock, tall columns with six sides, like honeycombs, but with smooth flat tops, and put them in the sea, making a great road of stepping stones. This stretched from Antrim in Ireland to Staffa in Scotland, and he proudly called it "The Giant's Causeway."

For many years Finn and his lovely wife, Oonagh, lived at home in peace. In his cave sat Bennadonner, staring out wistfully across the sea. He was lonely in his cave and he wanted a wife, too.

One stormy morning he sent a message across to Finn, challenging him to a fight, and saying he would be over to see him as soon as the sea was calm again, and not slopping over the Causeway. (No giant likes getting his feet wet, and Bennadonner couldn't swim either.)

Finn read the challenge to Oonagh, and they both roared with laughter. They shook so much that down in the village all the chimney pots fell off, and the people put up their shutters, against a storm. "Let him come!" laughed Finn, making a pen out of a small fir tree and scribbling a message on his wife's best table-cloth. "Let's fight! We'll soon see who's the stronger." And the meeting was fixed for the very next fine day.

Sure enough, one sunny morning Bennadonner set off for Antrim across the Giant's Causeway. Finn had gone for a walk before dinner, just a little stroll right across the Six Counties, so when Bennadonner reached his house the Irish giant was many miles from home.

Oonagh shouted to him across the mountains when she saw the Scottish giant prowling around the house, and Finn rushed back toward Antrim. His feet were so large that lakes formed where his shoes sank in the mud. He was looking forward to meeting puny Bennadonner, and to putting him in his place. But when he reached home he saw with horror that two huge footprints had been freshly made outside the door, *footprints at least as huge as his own!*

Finn shook with nerves, and the whole of Ireland trembled. This meant that Bennadonner was as big as he was! But how could this be? Wasn't Finn MacCool the biggest giant in the whole world? He sucked his magic thumb, but for once no bright idea came to him. So he hurried inside to ask his wife's advice.

"Stop sucking your thumb, Finn," she told him severely, and she set his dinner before him. This began with sixteen duck eggs, eight pigs' trotters, and three raw onions to help digest the meal. Then she brought in a piece of roast meat so huge it covered the whole table. But Finn wasn't hungry. All he could think of was Bennadonner skulking around outside in the darkness.

He was sucking his thumb again, and trying not to cry, when somebody knocked at the door so hard the whole house shook to its foundations. "It's Bennadonner!" he whimpered, clinging to Oonagh. "What am I going to do?"

His wife pulled out a cradle from under the table. It had once belonged to their son Ossian, but he'd long ago gone to live with the fairies, and was learning to be a poet. "Get into it!" she ordered, giving him a poke.

"I'm too big!" he protested.

"Well, you'll just have to double up," she said, stuffing him in, "or treble up." And she whisked a blanket over him as the door creaked open and Bennadonner strode into the room.

He was a horrible sight. He was every bit as big as the handsome red-haired Finn, who now lay squashed in the cradle by the fire, sucking his thumb, and trying to look like a baby. He was dressed in the skins of rats and skunks and he had a third eye in the middle of his forehead which rolled about hideously when he spoke.

"Where is Finn MacCool?" Bennadonner roared.

Oonagh was all sweetness. "He's out walking, Mr. Bennadonner," she said, "but he'll be back shortly. Sit yourself down, do, and let me offer you some food and drink."

She set a tankard of whiskey before him as big as a wash-tub, then went to the fire to turn over the flat round oaten cakes that she was cooking on an iron griddle. As she worked, the giant glanced at the gently rocking cradle. "That's a fine baby you have there, madam," he said.

"To be sure," she answered, "he's but a few weeks old, and no teeth yet."

Bennadonner, biting on his magic middle finger, suddenly knew that danger was near, and thought of Finn MacCool. "Where is your man?" he demanded more roughly. "Is he hiding from me?"

"*Hiding?*" Oonagh said scornfully. "My Finn *hide*? Why, he's twice the giant you are."

"Oh, *really*?" said Bennadonner, getting angrily to his feet. "I have three times his strength."

"Have you now?" Oonagh said coolly. "Could you turn my house around, for example?"

The giant went straight out into the darkness, lifted up the great stone house from its foundations, and turned it so that it faced the opposite way, with its back to the sea. While he was outside Oonagh slipped a spare griddle into one of the oaten cakes and fetched a freshly made white cheese from her dairy. She had plans to deal with Bennadonner. But Finn was less confident. He burrowed down into his blankets and sucked his magic thumb very hard.

"Have some oaten cakes, do, Mr. Bennadonner," Oonagh wheedled. He had turned the house around for sure, but she still believed she could outwit him and send him packing. The giant took a big bite and growled horribly, spitting out two teeth. "What kind of oaten cake is *this*?" he demanded.

"Oh, the softest and finest to be sure," purred Oonagh. "See, the baby likes it well enough." Into Finn's hand she slipped a piece of oaten cake that had no griddle iron in it. He munched it up in a flash, and made gurgling baby noises.

Bennadonner's mouth dropped open. What kind of baby could this be? "But you said he had no *teeth*," he spluttered, "and your oaten cakes are as hard as iron."

"I did surely," Oonagh said easily, "and he has not. But his little gums are hard. Here, feel for yourself," and she thrust the giant's right hand into Finn's mouth.

He promptly bit off Bennadonner's magic finger. "Aargh!" roared Bennadonner, hopping about in pain, "It's no baby in that cradle, madam, it's a fiend!"

"Indeed, 'tis nothing but a baby. But he's strong, sir, like his father. Let me show you. He can squeeze water out of a stone."

Into Finn's hand she slipped the round white cheese, new from the dairy, and as he squeezed it, the whey dripped down.

Bennadonner's three eyes bulged in his head, and he immediately tried to do the same. But cunning Oonagh had given him a white stone, and all he managed to do was to break his remaining fingers.

This was too much for the Scottish giant. If Finn MacCool's baby was as strong as this, what must the father be like? He turned and ran out of the house, down to the shore and tore back to Staffa just as fast as he could, across the Giant's Causeway. But as he did so, he ripped up the great slippery stones and flung them into the sea. He didn't want Finn MacCool to come visiting *him*.

And that is why there are only two bits of the Causeway left now — on Staffa, in Scotland, and in Ireland, on the rocky Antrim coast. You can go and look at them for yourself, if you don't believe me.

If you should see them, remember this: you'd still be able to walk right across the Irish sea, without getting your feet wet, if it weren't for those two giants who couldn't swim.

HOW PERSEUS KILLED THE GORGON

A Greek Myth

In the ancient Greek city of Tiryns there lived a king named Acrisius. He had one child, a beautiful daughter named Danae, but he wanted a son to make sure that his kingdom would be fearlessly defended after he died.

Messengers were sent to Delphi, where the famous oracle, a prophetess, sometimes told people what would happen in the future. They heard from her that no son would ever be born to King Acrisius, but that he would one day have a grandson, who would kill him.

The king was terrified and declared that the lovely Danae must never marry. To make absolutely certain, he walled her up in a tower of solid brass. When the sun shone down on it, people marveled at its beauty, but at night their hearts were torn out of them by the terrible weeping of the king's daughter deep inside.

Acrisius could keep human beings away from Danae, but he had no power against the gods. Zeus himself visited her, falling down upon the tower in a shower of golden rain, and they fell in love. In time a son was born to her, and she called him Perseus.

Now that he had a grandson, Acrisius's fears turned to madness. He ordered carpenters to make a huge wooden chest, and when it was ready he placed Danae in it, with

the new-born Perseus in her arms. His servants carried the chest down to the sea, and it was pushed out into the waves. Acrisius dared not kill his daughter and grandson outright, because he knew that the gods would punish him. But he hoped that the chest would fill with water, and that they would perish at sea.

The chest bobbed away, and eventually the watchers on the shore lost sight of it. Night came, the wind started howling, and Danae clutched the baby to her, praying that their lives might be spared. When the sun rose next day, she found that they had been washed up on an island. It was called Seriphos, and a king named Polydectes ruled over it. His brother Dictys was only a fisherman, and it was he who found the great chest on the beach, took Danae and the baby home, and cared for them as his own family.

Perseus grew up into a strong and handsome young man, and his mother Danae, though aging, remained very beautiful. King Polydectes wanted to take her away from Dictys to the royal palace. But he was a cruel man, and she would have nothing to do with him. In the end he decided he would take her by force, but the problem was her son Perseus, who went with her everywhere to defend her. He must be gotten rid of.

So the king gave a great banquet, and to this feast all the young men of the island promised to bring gifts. Perseus had nothing to offer, but, goaded by Polydectes, he rashly promised to bring him whatever he desired.

"Bring me the head of Medusa, the fiercest of the Gorgons," the king said cleverly, knowing that Perseus would never come back from such a mission, for whoever looked into Medusa's monstrous face was turned into stone.

All around Perseus, people were laughing and jeering at his foolish promise, but he lifted up his voice and cried, "I *will* bring you the Gorgon's head, or I'll die in the attempt!"

As he sat alone, wondering how on earth he could carry out his vow, two of the gods came to him, offering help. Hermes, their messenger, gave him the sharpest sword in the world, and the lovely Athena gave him a polished shield. "You must not look into Medusa's face," she told him. "Look into this instead, and you will see her reflection, and be spared. Now go. Seek first the Three Gray Sisters. They will tell you how to find the Nymphs who live at the back of the North Wind. They will provide you with all you need to find the Gorgons and kill Medusa." And taking Hermes' hand, she vanished from sight.

After many days Perseus reached the lonely cave where

the Three Gray Sisters lived. They were the daughters of the giant Phorcus and they were hideous to look upon. From birth they had been old women with lank gray hair, and with only one eye and one tooth to share between them.

Perseus crept up silently behind them as they sat gabbling to one another in the mouth of the cave, snatched the single eye from their fingers and said, "Daughters of Phorcus, I have robbed you of your sight. Tell me how to find the Nymphs who dwell at the back of the North Wind, or I will leave you in darkness forever."

Then the old women wailed and moaned, begging for their eye again, but he would not restore it to them until they had told him the secret of the Nymphs. Once he knew the way, he tossed the eye back to them, and left them fighting for it, as he sped off along the stony track.

The Nymphs of the North Wind welcomed him, and he spent many days in their leafy paradise.

"I must find Medusa," he told them, "and carry her head to Polydectes. Help me, I pray you. No man can do such a thing alone."

They dared not go with him, but they gave him three gifts, the Shoes of Swiftness, a magic bag in which to put the Gorgon's head, and the Cap of Darkness which makes all who wear it invisible.

It was a terrible journey to the land where the three Gorgons lived. All along the winding road Perseus saw pathetic statues of men and animals, living, breathing creatures that had been turned into stone by Medusa. She was the most dangerous of the three, but she had once been a mortal, and so Perseus could kill her, if only he could get near enough, without her eyes being turned upon him. Her two sisters were immortal, and he feared them too, knowing that they might rip him to pieces with their fiendish nails of brass.

At last he was in sight of the Gorgons' lair. There they lay, twined together in sleep, but the snakes that grew from their heads hissed and writhed as they sensed a stranger approaching, and the sun shone on their scaly dragon skin, and on the great gold wings that sprouted from their shoulders.

Putting on the Cap of Darkness, Perseus drew close to Medusa, holding Athena's shield in front of him. There, as in a mirror, he saw the awful face, and drawing Hermes' marvelous sword from its scabbard, he sliced off the Gorgon's head with a single blow.

Hideous screams went up from Medusa's sisters, and they clawed at him as he put the head, with its angry snakes still writhing and hissing, into the Nymphs' magic bag. Quickly

he buckled on the Shoes of Swiftness and rose into the air, away from the screaming monsters as they wept over the dead Medusa, away from the stony valley with its sorrowing statues, away to the deserts and oceans of the world. He held the magic bag firmly by its strong silken strings, but as he flew, great drops of blood fell from it, magic blood, staining the sand far below. And wherever the blood fell a green oasis grew and flourished. You can see them there in the desert wastes to this day.

Night fell, and Perseus flew on and on into the first rays of the sun as it dawned upon the vast glittering sea that now rolled beneath his feet. Far below he saw a statue cut out of a rock, the figure of the most beautiful woman he had ever seen. He flew down, and as he got nearer, he saw that it was no statue but a real girl, and she was weeping. She was chained to the rock, and the rising tide was washing around her feet.

It was Andromeda, whose foolish mother, Cassiopeia, had boasted to the sea gods about her daughter's great beauty. To punish her they had raised up a monster from the waves who was laying waste all the kingdoms round about, killing innocent men and women and bringing mighty floods upon their growing crops. King Cepheus, Andromeda's father, had chained his daughter to the rock as a sacrifice to the furious creature, hoping its anger would cease.

Perseus took off the Cap of Darkness and appeared before the weeping girl in his own shape. In that moment the monster's head reared up out of the waves and its great jaws opened wide. Taking the bag, Perseus thrust the face

of Medusa toward the slavering creature, and at once it turned into a great ridge of gray rock, with the sea lapping gently all around it.

Great was the rejoicing at the royal palace of King Cepheus, and he willingly gave Perseus Andromeda's hand in marriage. They stayed there feasting for many days, but at last Perseus's thoughts turned to his home on the island of Seriphos. It was time to present Medusa's head to Polydectes.

Taking his new bride with him, Perseus set sail for Greece. But great was his anger when he reached Seriphos and found that his mother had been made a slave by Polydectes, and that Dictys, the kindly fisherman, had been thrown into prison. Perseus marched to the palace and found the king laughing and drinking with his friends. They all jeered at him when he walked into the great hall, and the king said sneeringly, "Well, look who's turned up, that fool Perseus who said he was going to kill the Gorgon!"

"And so I have," Perseus answered quietly. "The head is here," and he held up the magic bag.

"Show it to me," roared Polydectes drunkenly, draining down another cup of wine. It was clear that nobody in the hall believed a word of what the young man had said.

And so, holding it by its snaky hair, Perseus held aloft the head of Medusa for all to see. A sudden silence fell upon the revelers. There was no more clinking of goblets or banging of plates, no more yelling at the servants for more food and wine. All who had gazed into those terrible eyes had been turned into lumps of stone.

Dictys the fisherman became king of Seriphos, and Danae became his queen, and with Andromeda at his side Perseus set sail again, this time for the kingdom of Argolis. On the way, however, they stopped in Larissa. Great games were being held there, and the young hero wanted to try his skill at discus throwing.

Everyone there marveled at his power, but after his second throw a cry went up. The heavy iron disk had struck a glancing blow to the head of an old man who was watching, and he fell down dead. This was Acrisius, Perseus's own grandfather, who had lived all his life in fear of the prophecy that he would have a grandson who would one day bring about his own death.

Perseus reached Argolis in great sorrow and ruled there, with Andromeda as his queen, for the rest of his life. His deeds were great, and his bravery known throughout all the world. When they died Zeus, king of the gods, set him and his queen in heaven, and they became two stars.

Other books by Ann Pilling and Kady MacDonald Denton:

THE KINGFISHER BOOK OF BIBLE STORIES
Ann Pilling
Illustrated by Kady MacDonald Denton

•

A KINGFISHER TREASURY OF BIBLE STORIES, POEMS, AND PRAYERS FOR BEDTIME
Ann Pilling
Illustrated by Kady MacDonald Denton

•

A CHILD'S TREASURY OF NURSERY RHYMES
Kady MacDonald Denton

•

IN THE LIGHT OF THE MOON & OTHER BEDTIME STORIES
Sam McBratney
Illustrated by Kady MacDonald Denton